Serving as a counselor now for twe of the most complicated issues to restorative process that unfolds when a marriage becomes devastated by adultery. *After an Affair* is a much needed, insightful, and practical guide that will assist counselors and couples on the critical steps essential to restoring trust and intimacy when the horrors of infidelity have fractured the marriage covenant. Every pastor and counselor, or any couple trying to heal the emotional carnage resulting from adultery will cherish and be nurtured by the wisdom and insight offered in this excellent booklet. Loved the booklet!!

— Jeremy Lelek, PhD
  President, Association of Biblical Counselors

My review of this book leaves me with two words: Real and relevant!

— Dennis D. Frey, ThD
  President, Master's International University of Divinity, Evansville, IN

Howard Eyrich has long been my "go to" guy on a number of subjects. I can now add Marriage Rebuilding to my list. This is a remarkably helpful booklet, full of biblical strategies for the counselor to consider as he seeks to help marriage partners through the darkest hour of their lives. Counselor, do not wait until you are faced with a rebuilding situation to read this booklet. Read it now and be prepared for the opportunity that will surely be yours to minister the Word to a hurting couple.

— Donn R. Arms
  Institute for Nouthetic Studies, Simpsonville, SC

After an Affair is an extremely rich resource for couples who find themselves in the aftermath of infidelity. The authors offer biblical wisdom and down-to-earth, practical experience gleaned from working with numerous couples for several decades. This booklet reminded me of why I love biblical counseling and I am grateful to have these incredible insights from seasoned practitioners who practice what they proclaim.

— Mark E. Shaw, DMin
   Author of 20 publications
   President, Truth in Love Ministries, Indianapolis, IN
   Founder, The Addiction Connection

Contemporary, practical, and most importantly, biblical. Following the prescription laid out in this booklet should go a long way to helping couples who experience an affair to rebuild trust and the marriage relationship.

— Pastor Bob Froese, PhD
   Senior Pastor, Faith Fellowship Church, Clarence, NY
   Executive Board Member, IABC

After an Affair: Rebuilding Your Trust; Rebuilding Your Marriage
© 2018 Howard Eyrich

ISBN-13: 978-1986736435
ISBN-10: 1986736431

All rights reserved. No part of this publication may be reproduced or transmitted in any form or by any means without written permission from the publisher.

All scriptures are taken from The Holy Bible, English Standard Version®, copyright © 2001 by Crossway, 2011 Text Edition. Used by permission. All rights reserved.

Published by Growth Advantage Communication, LLC
3867 James Hill Circle
Hoover, Alabama 35226
growthadvantage@gmail.com

DEDICATION

This booklet is dedicated to all those who have allowed us to be part of God's healing their marriages. They have been our teachers in the process.

Table of Contents

Words of Appreciation 9
Introduction 11
Thirteen Strategies Essential to Rebuilding Trust 13
   Strategy One—Truth-Telling is Trust Building 16
   Strategy Two—Radical Amputation is Emancipation 18
   Strategy Three—Owning Your Sin Produces Humble
      Compassion 21
   Strategy Four—Submit to Scrutiny 24
   Strategy Five—Practice Patience in the Face of
      Rejection... 26
   Strategy Six—Six Degrees of Connection............................... 28
   Strategy Seven—Re-prioritizing Your Spouse 31
   Strategy Eight—Dispel Doubt with an Open Life.................. 34
   Strategy Nine—Dissipate Stress by Wise Choices.................. 36
   Strategy Ten—Dispense with Facebook, Twitter and
      Instagram... 38
   Strategy Eleven—Engage in a Spiritual Journey 40
   Strategy Twelve—Rebuilding Trust Flows from
      Rebuilding the Relationship... 42
   Strategy Thirteen—Trust Can Flourish in
      Worshiping and Ministering Together 45
   Conclusion 47
Rebuilding the Relationship After the Affair 49
   Jesus' Solution for Rebuilding the Relationship...................... 51
      Initiatives: Ten Practical Steps 55
   Paul's Rules for Maintaining A Relationship 59

 Rule One: Stop Lying and Start Truth-Telling 59
 Rule Two: Be Relationship-Focused Not Issue-Focused 60
 Rule Three: Attack the Problem Not Your Spouse 61
 Rule Four: Don't React, Pro-Act 62
 Rule Five: Listen Before You Speak or Get Angry 64
Our Strong Suggestion 66
Appendix 67
About the Authors 69
Also by Dr. Howard Eyrich 71
Scripture References 72

WORDS OF APPRECIATION

Any written work is not the product of one person. This booklet is not an exception. First, I would give credit to the writers of many blogs, sacred and secular, that I perused on this subject. I did not read them so much as research, but rather to saturate my mind with the nuances of the subject. Many of the ideas contained herein have shown up in one way or another in numerous pieces I have read. As the writer of Ecclesiastes observed, there is nothing new under the sun. To each contributor I say, "Thank you for sparking the desire to create a document rooted in theology to address this thorny issue in a practical manner. This work would be less without you." Originally, I wrote this to provide a handout for use in our counseling office.

I want to thank Shirley Crowder whose multiple talents, not only as an editor but also in the administration of our summer training program for many years, has blessed and expanded my ministry. I want to thank Leigh Ann Reese whose computer skills brought the original booklet to print. Then there is Tami Wells and Nedia Rooker, my administrative assistants, who kept my crazy life orderly. Finally, I want to thank my colleague, Dr. Cheryl Blackmon, who invested numerous hours of her personal time in this project.

INTRODUCTION

▼▼▼▼▼▼▼▼▼▼▼▼▼▼▼▼▼▼▼

"I can't believe you did this!" shouted Mary. "You are a sorry specimen of a Christian man! How could you do this to me and your children—and with my best friend! Oh, was that ever a slip of the tongue. My best friend would not sleep with my husband!"

Mary ranted on for hours. By two in the morning, she was exhausted and fell asleep. Ronnie sat on the chaise lounge dazed by his wife's torrent of wrath and belittling.

"How did I get here? This dear woman is the best thing that ever happened to me. Oh, dear God, I have played King David and my own son the role of Nathan, the prophet! Lord, how did I get here? Why did you let me do this?"

▲▲▲▲▲▲▲▲▲▲▲▲▲▲▲▲▲▲▲▲▲

Is recovery from this disaster possible? Yes, it is. This booklet is about rebuilding trust, then rebuilding and maintaining a marriage. Herein we assume the importance of repentance as essential and proceed from that foundation to essentials of rebuilding and maintaining the marriage.

The discovery of infidelity—whether it entails secret text messages, sexting, phone conversations, internet exchanges, long-term extra-marital relationships, or even same sex attraction and engagement—can be devastating. Cheating on a spouse and lying to cover it up naturally breeds distrust and suspicion.

A couple can, however, rebuild trust. The speed and degree of recovery are greatly affected by the actions of the spouse who cheated. However, many offenders do not understand the feelings of the betrayed spouses and have no idea how to rebuild trust. The following practical strategies rooted in biblical theology will help those who have cheated and who are serious about rebuilding trust and healing their marital relationships. Rebuilding begins with repentance and forgiveness and the rapidity of recovery is proportional to the thoroughness of each.

Please Note Two Things:
1. As you read you will find many examples which are slices of real cases. All names and locations are fictitious, and confidentiality is ensured since my counseling experience transpired in eight cites scattered across the eastern United States over a span of more than forty years. For each case cited there are multiple others with great similarities.
2. When Scripture passages occur with the strategy heading, read the passage before reading the strategy, as they generally support the strategy. When Scripture references occur in the text, they are specific to the point at which they are inserted.

Thirteen Strategies Essential to Rebuilding Trust

The following strategies for rebuilding trust in a marital relationship are based upon various passages in the Bible. For example, Strategy One is drawn directly from Ephesians 4:25. Running through these strategies is the recognition of the importance of personal responsibility for one's sinful choices. Again, honesty and transparency, common character traits cited in Scripture, play a prominent role.

Furthermore, confession (owning one's sin) and forgiveness (a decision and a promise to not dwell on the offense, talk about it to others, or throw it up to the spouse later), which are the foundation for rebuilding the marriage, must precede these strategies. Yet, confession and forgiveness will also be a process. The offender will remember details or be questioned about aspects of the affair, and in the process, realize that deeper confession is necessary. As well, the offended party will find himself or herself retracing the act/hurt and having to choose to forgive another detail.

STRATEGY ONE

Truth-Telling is Trust Building

Stop lying and start truth-telling (Ephesians 4:25)! Betraying your spouse's trust by your infidelity is only complicated by lying. Twisting the truth, hiding details, or denying even the slightest detail does what my mother told me when she caught me lying (Proverbs 12:22): "It adds insult to injury."

Honesty is the beginning of recovery from an affair. Honesty is the means for reestablishing your integrity, and integrity is foundational to rebuilding trust (Ephesians 5:7-16).

Commit yourself to becoming trustworthy. Pledge yourself to honesty—truth-telling. Do not plead for his or her trust; but do affirm that you desire that he or she trust you again. Begin with an unrestrained confession stating a willingness to tell as much detail as he or she is ready to hear (Proverbs 28:13).

Stick to facts. Even though you may desire to protect your spouse, honesty is necessary. Do not *sugarcoat* your sin. Allow your spouse to determine the level of detail he or she desires to hear. You cannot deal with your guilt and your spouse cannot deal with his or her hurt and anger without full disclosure. In the short-term truth hurts, but in the long-term truth provides opportunity for reconciliation (Psalm 51:6, 10).

Once you have told the truth, keep telling the truth. When your spouse asks why you were an hour late getting home from the office, do not say, "The boss called me into his office as I was leaving," unless that is the truth. If you stopped to look at the new ring you are planning to present to your spouse to affirm your commitment, you need to declare it.

For all you know your boss may have called your home thirty minutes earlier to ask you a question. Your spouse is listening to see if you will be truthful. Alternatively, your spouse may read your body language and know when you are lying

One final thought regarding the complications of lying: If you lie again, even with the very best intentions, your momentary hesitancy will often give you away (1 John 1:5-7).

▼▼▼▼▼▼▼▼▼▼▼▼▼▼▼▼▼▼▼

"The problem with being a police officer is that you know when someone is lying," said John as he sent his partner off to investigate a lead. "I have another interrogation to conduct." He then turned to his wife and began to question her regarding a friend's social media postings that placed his wife somewhere other than where she had said she was while he was away for several days on an investigation. She began to cry.

"I did not tell you that I had been to that party because I knew it would upset you. We've been doing so well! I did not want to spoil it. I only went there because Claire called me to come get her. She had too much to drink and did not want to drive home. When I walked in Darlene hugged me and told me she had missed me. Jim snapped that picture. I am so sorry I lied. I should not have even gone to get Claire. I should have called her dad. They both would have been mad, but that would be better than your being mad."

"You are so right! If you want me to learn to trust you, you cannot even come close to a lie. Remember, I do this stuff for a living. I know when someone is lying even if I am not looking for it. Are we clear?" John asked with a resolute tone.

▲▲▲▲▲▲▲▲▲▲▲▲▲▲▲▲▲▲▲

Strategy Two

Radical Amputation[1] is Emancipation

Make a clean break with your consort (James 4:17)! You lit a fire! That person has feelings for you. Unless there is an unequivocal disengagement, it is quite likely that you will be pursued. This person is an integral part of the problem. When emails or text messages show up on your phone, there will be more pain and anger for your spouse to process. You may feel like a blunt breakup will hurt the other person's feelings. It will! If you are not frank and pointed when asserting finality, your spouse will be hurt. The bottom line is this: Everybody is going to be hurt. The real question is which relationship will be healed (Matthew 5:23-24; Proverbs 14:12)?

So how is unequivocal disengagement done? It is best to do this by speakerphone with your spouse present. It may sound like this: "Mary, this is Jim. You need to know that my wife is sitting here with me and we are on speakerphone. I need to tell you that I have sinned against God, my wife, my family, and you by having this affair with you. I am making this call in her presence so that she can hear me ask for your forgiveness and tell you that this affair is over. I deeply regret my sin. God has convicted me and forgiven me. Mary has forgiven me. My children have forgiven me. I desire your forgiveness because I want to close this chapter of my life. I want to encourage you to seek your husband's forgiveness and reconcile your marriage." This call may be even more difficult if the other person did not know you were cheating—that person thought you had

---

[1] Jay Adams modeled utilizing this term in this manner. He drew upon Jesus from Matthew 5:30ff.

integrity. Whatever the case, in the long run, it is a necessary strategy of restoring trust with your spouse.

If the affair was with a coworker, remember that your day-to-day encounters with him or her may make rebuilding trust very difficult for your spouse. Get your life priorities straight and do what you need to do (Psalm 1:1-2) to put this affair behind you. You may need to ask for a transfer to another department—even if it means a cut in salary. You may need to seek another position if your spouse requests that you do so (Mark 9:43).

Displaying the breakup in the presence of your spouse helps you communicate that he or she is more important than the other man or woman. Do not underestimate the value of this action (Ephesians 5:8-17).

▼▼▼▼▼▼▼▼▼▼▼▼▼▼▼▼▼▼▼▼

Michael and Jane had been friends since junior high school, and during their senior year had a serious romantic relationship. They went to different colleges in different states. Their relationship cooled, and each fell in love with and married other people. Early in the marriage, Michael spoke of Jane on occasions to Mary.

"It bothers me a bit when you talk about Jane. I would appreciate it if we could leave her out of our lives," Mary told Michael over a dinner date one night. That was twenty years ago. Other than the discovery of a couple of pictures of Jane that were stowed in Michael's gun safe, which generated a heated discussion, Jane had not been part of their lives since then.

Michael received a promotion to national sales manager. Since his company was a small, targeted business, his territory comprised the major cities in the U.S. Over the years, he had secretly seen Jane occasionally on business trips. Her company serviced the same clients, but with other products. A couple of years earlier she had divorced, and she and Michael had begun having an occasional dinner together when they were in the same city on business. Michael did not know that Mary's second cousin, whom Mary seldom saw and hardly knew, worked for the same company as Jane, but sold a different product line to a common customer base.

She called Mary and said, "Look, I don't want to cause trouble and you may be aware of this, but I've seen your husband on several occasions in different cities having dinner with a co-worker of mine." Mary asked her for a description and realized it was Jane.

An ugly affair was uncovered. Michael and Mary engaged in counseling. After several multiple-hour counseling sessions, Mary gave Michael an ultimatum: "Lose the job and Jane or lose me!" For Mary, radical amputation was the only solution to ensure that Michael would not have contact with Jane (Matthew 18:8).

▲▲▲▲▲▲▲▲▲▲▲▲▲▲▲▲▲

Sometimes it takes such a radical decision to save your marriage. Taking this action says to your spouse, "I am serious. I have hurt you tremendously. I am willing to pay the price necessary to re-engage you in our marriage."

STRATEGY THREE
Owning Your Sin Produces Humble Compassion

Cheating is 100% wrong! It comes from a sense of entitlement. In the language of popular culture, "it is about getting my needs met." It is pure selfishness. Own it as such! Rebuilding trust is about selflessly doing everything in your power to help your spouse feel safe in the relationship (James 1:12-17).

Even if your spouse is guilty of mistakes (and/or sin) that provoked you, do not blame your spouse for your cheating. Instead of cheating, there were many options open to you for addressing the issues. If you are blaming your spouse for your sin, you are admitting that you are not honest. This is not the time to discuss your spouse's transgressions. During the reconciliation process there will be opportunity to explore these issues. Your choice to cheat and lie was not because of his or her mistakes, it was your own lustful desires that produced your sinful choice (James 4:1-3).

If you are expecting sympathy, you are being foolish (Proverbs 26:4-5). Your spouse may have been dissatisfied and discouraged with the relationship as well, but your spouse made the decision to not cheat on you, nor to lie to you, nor act with insolent pride (Proverbs 21:24).

Bogus excuses abound by those who cheat. They are legion. As a counselor, here are a few that I have heard: she seduced me, the strong attraction to him confused me (said regarding her male trainer), I can't explain it—it just happened, temptation was strong and unexpected, we were in bed before I realized what was happening, etc. You made a series of choices that led to the grand choice. You had many opportunities to say no and you did not! This reality magnifies your spouse's hurt.

A counselor friend observed, "What amazes me is how quickly a cheater gets defensive when his sin is on the table." Your best defense is a good offense. That good offense is humility expressed with regret and remorse, coupled with compassion for your hurt spouse, and expressed with genuine tears (James 4:5-12).

▼▼▼▼▼▼▼▼▼▼▼▼▼▼▼▼▼▼▼▼

Jim turned to Sally and tentatively touched her hand. With tears streaming down his face he said, "Sally, I have been so wrong. I have behaved like King David. I betrayed my dear friend, Ken. I have betrayed Jennifer by seducing her. I have betrayed you more than them. Most of all I have betrayed my Savior and Lord. I have already sought His forgiveness earlier this afternoon with Pastor Jones. Now I am asking you to forgive me, and then with you on the phone I want to call Ken and Jennifer and seek their forgiveness. Sally, will you please forgive me?"

▲▲▲▲▲▲▲▲▲▲▲▲▲▲▲▲▲▲▲▲

▼▼▼▼▼▼▼▼▼▼▼▼▼▼▼▼▼▼▼▼

Over the last forty years, I have had the joy of seeing a number of folks walk through this process. One was Susan. She came to tell me she no longer loved her husband and wanted to divorce him. After some listening and questioning, I looked at her and said, "Please allow me to ask you a very important question. Have you had an affair?" Susan began to sob and admitted that she had done so. We arranged for her husband, Richard, to attend the next session and she agreed to own her sin and to seek his forgiveness. That is exactly what she did. Richard almost went into a state of shock, but by God's grace, I led him through the process of accepting the reality and granting her forgiveness. The following Christmas I received a card from them. Their family picture graced the card underscored by these words: "Thanks to your counsel and the grace of God, our family is together and growing both spiritually and numerically" (she was pregnant).

▲▲▲▲▲▲▲▲▲▲▲▲▲▲▲▲▲▲▲▲

Owning your sin[2] and seeking forgiveness is the beginning of your spouse's ability to rebuild trust.

---

[2] This is a non-theological way of describing repentance.

Strategy Four

Submit to Scrutiny

(Zechariah 8:15-17; Romans 12:16-18)

Ouch! That question hurts. You should expect questions that will strip you of your pride and unmask your duplicity. You have compromised your privacy. You agreed to give up your privacy when you said, "I do." Your privacy and your so-called rights got you into this situation. Now your spouse is going to examine the details of your life with a fine-toothed comb. Your spouse may ask the same questions repeatedly and will cross-reference your stories. You may wonder if you married a detective. If you are not truthful, your spouse will find it out.

▼▼▼▼▼▼▼▼▼▼▼▼▼▼▼▼▼▼

"You told me that you only met her at that gorgeous hotel that you never had the money to take me to! Now I find this receipt under your car seat for three Holiday Inns. So, what were you doing at the Holiday Inns? When I asked you about that trip to Mobile, you gave me that phony tale that the boss asked you to try to get back the customer that she lost. I need to have straight answers. I need to know exactly what you were doing at each of these hotels and the purpose of your trips and I want something by which I can verify your answers."

▲▲▲▲▲▲▲▲▲▲▲▲▲▲▲▲▲▲

Questions (e.g., Was she pretty? Was he sexy? Was she a good conversationalist? Was this just about sex?) may really be the expression of your spouse's insecurities generated by your betrayal. In response to such questions, you must not lie but rather take them as opportunities to affirm your spouse and his or her special characteristics—to *overcome evil with good* (Romans 12:21). You should recall the good qualities of your earlier relationship, repent over your failure to appreciate them, and express your desire to experience again those dimensions of your relationship (Revelation 2:1-7).

▼▼▼▼▼▼▼▼▼▼▼▼▼▼▼▼▼▼▼

I did a post-affair recommitment counseling session. Rachael had committed adultery. After several months, she had repented, sought forgiveness from Augustine, confessed her sin before the church, who all knew about it, and sought forgiveness from her fellow Christians.

Augustine was somewhat obsessive compulsive. He tracked her every move. He reviewed her phone records and emails. He could recall every conversation and identify the slightest discrepancy. I had no doubt that his behavior contributed to Rachael's desire for her consort. In rebuilding trust, however, Rachael found it necessary to embrace Augustine's questioning. Over time, he needed to learn how to put parameters on his obsessive habit. Nevertheless, in the rebuilding process Rachael learned to indulge his questions with honest and full answers.

▲▲▲▲▲▲▲▲▲▲▲▲▲▲▲▲▲▲▲▲

STRATEGY FIVE

Practice Patience in the Face of Rejection

Choose to practice patience while your spouse works at choosing to trust you again. Most writers on this subject talk about your need to earn trust. I prefer to speak of choosing to live in such a manner that you engender a desire in your spouse to choose to trust you again (Psalm 27:13-14; Psalm 26:6-7; 1 Corinthians 13:4-8).

Remember, you have supplied the evidence for the prosecution. Now you must supply the evidence to support a pardon. Confession, apology, seeking forgiveness, and renewing your vow to remain faithful are not sufficient to motivate your spouse to immediately return the relationship to normal.

Not only will the relationship take time to return to normal, but other dimensions of life will take time as well. Emotions will bounce. One day your spouse will be smiling, and all will seem well, but two days later, she will be crying, or he will be angry. Undoubtedly, there will be anxiety and sleep loss. You will be having a normal conversation and unexpectedly your spouse will zap you with a sharp barb.

Be patient as your spouse goes through the process (James 1:2-4, 1 Corinthians 13:4-8). Do not dictate the length of time it should take your spouse to be over it, and do not demand a time frame. Instead, do all that you can to allay his or her fears and check in with him or her periodically to find out if he or she are copacetic (Galatians 5:22ff).

Your relationship during this time is not necessarily an indicator of how it will be from now on. Your spouse's suspicion and distrust can eventually dissipate when you are providing the appropriate evidence.

▼▼▼▼▼▼▼▼▼▼▼▼▼▼▼▼▼▼▼▼

"Sometimes I just don't want to be around you. You turn my stomach! I certainly do not want you touching me unless I give you permission!" This was Megan's outburst in response to John's attempt to hug her when he came home from work.

His counselor cautioned him about reacting to this rejection. He encouraged John to be patient and gentle with Megan. "For a while her emotions are going to be erratic. You will have to pray for patience. You will have to rehearse how you will respond," cautioned his pastor. "She has forgiven you. But, like my wife said once when I deeply hurt her and sought her forgiveness, 'I will forgive you, but you need to give me time to get used to it.'"

▲▲▲▲▲▲▲▲▲▲▲▲▲▲▲▲▲▲▲▲

STRATEGY SIX

Six Degrees of Connection

There are six degrees of connection that are essential in this fight to regain trust.

1. **Availability**. Your spouse cannot process this pain if you are not available for conversation. Physical presence proclaims that you value him or her (Philippians 2:1-7; Philippians 1:9-11). Offer to receive text messages whenever your spouse feels the need or wants to make contact. Be sure to provide opportunity for at least thirty minutes of uninterrupted personal communication in which you give your spouse your full attention.

2. **Attentiveness**. Your spouse lost the most important person in his or her life. That loss in most instances began long before the affair. The affair happened, in part, because the two of you became disconnected. Now you need to reconnect. You should be there to listen when your spouse weeps or bemoans the pain and the losses. You do not need to counsel or even console. You do need to listen and affirm the agony. Randomly surprise your spouse with a phone call to simply say, "I've been thinking of you and I love you." (Proverbs 18:13)

3. **Amplification.** Early in the recovery process, you will need to be there to fill in the blanks, to explain the gaps in the story. By explaining, you help your spouse avoid speculation. Television shows and tabloids will fuel the worst-case scenarios. (Proverbs 13:15)

4. **Affirming**. Remember, you generated the situation that gives rise to a raging river, driving a load of debris in the form of questions and ugly emotions. Being longsuffering and patient allows the storm to pass and

the river to calm. Be prepared for your spouse to grow weary and to express a desire to end the relationship. Patiently affirming your spouse's frustration while also expressing your desire to redeem your marriage will go a long way toward calming those troubled waters and generating a desire to join you in rebuilding your marriage. (Proverbs 13:21)

5. **Appearance**. Any time it is necessary to spend time with the opposite sex, your spouse may struggle with suspicion. Do not try to combat this with accusations of paranoia. Confirm that you understand. Explain the purpose of the activity. Give the details about where you will be going. Be specific about who will be involved in the project or activity. Describe the safeguards you have built into the situation to avoid even the appearance of evil. Be sure you build them in before you inform your spouse of the necessary encounter. (Proverbs 2:1-22)

6. **Avoidance**. Being smart with your smart phone is being wise. Give your spouse all passwords and permission to examine it at any time. The same is true for your computer. If it is a business computer, sit down with your spouse and go through the email daily. Scripture tells us to avoid even the appearance of evil. Take heed to this exhortation. Avoid association with people, places and sites that will give the appearance of entanglement evil.[3] (2 Timothy 2:22)

---

[3] One commentator rightly observes that 1 Thessalonians 5:22 does not teach us to avoid the appearance of evil (something that may look questionable but is innocent). Rather, it teaches us to avoid evil at its every appearance, or in whatever form it manifests itself. He is correct. This is precisely our intent in this exhortation.

▼▼▼▼▼▼▼▼▼▼▼▼▼▼▼▼▼▼

Sam was unfaithful and sought forgiveness, but he did not implement the above suggestions. His wife forgave him and extended trust even though their relationship had been tenuous for several years prior to the affair. Sam traveled weekly for his job and frequently had to engage with female clients and staff. Six months after the affair, Sarah was pressing Sam on some emails he had deleted before she was able to read them. He resented her intrusion and left home without a resolution to the blow-up.

Following three days of meetings, Sam pulled out of the parking lot behind a woman who had been flirting with him during the meetings. When she turned off for her hotel, he followed. The next week Sam and Sarah were back in counseling with trust destroyed. He had failed to be patient and had acted foolishly out of anger. (Proverbs 1:20-33; Proverbs 5:1-14)

▲▲▲▲▲▲▲▲▲▲▲▲▲▲▲▲▲▲

STRATEGY SEVEN

Re-prioritizing Your Spouse

(Ephesians 4:1-6; Colossians 3:12-17)

Imagine where your spouse saw himself or herself on your priority list when the affair became known. Obviously, your spouse was not number one! Imagine what you would be thinking if the circumstances were reversed. Imagine what your mutual friends would be thinking. "Boy, he sure sees her as a piece of junk." They would not have seen you acting with all humility and gentleness, with patience, bearing with one another in love, eager to maintain the unity of the Spirit in the bond of peace (Ephesians 4:2-3).

You will now need to engage in the process of restoring your spouse to the place of number one in your life. It now becomes your challenge to generate in your spouse the belief that you will not cheat again.

Explore your mindset by answering some important questions. For what reasons did I fail to appreciate my spouse? What traits delighted me about him or her in the beginning of our relationship? What did I do to extinguish those traits? What can I do to restore them in my spouse? How can I help my spouse regain an accurate self-image? (Romans 12:3)

Answering these questions will help you be practical in the trust building enterprise. Create a list of the things that are special about your spouse. Explore creative ways to affirm these traits. Make and execute concrete plans that demonstrate you really do value him or her.

As my mother, and probably your mother, used to say, "Actions speak louder than words." Your choices communicated the lack of love. You must now choose to demonstrate your love. However, do not be surprised if your spouse questions the genuineness of your actions—after all, you were a liar and you did not display love!

Humiliation is a major factor for the victim. You have sinned. You feel humiliated by your sin. Nevertheless, your spouse is the victim and that humiliation is far greater. Forgiving you and even considering reconciliation is humiliating. Do not underestimate this horrible emotion. As playwright William Congreve observed in *The Mourning Bride* in 1697, "Heaven has no rage like love to hatred turned, nor hell a fury like a woman scorned." Congreve may have been a bit prejudice here since I have seen men take up the same response. So, be patient and supportive.

Giving or receiving affection may be particularly difficult. Again, patience is the byword. You will have to wait until your spouse is ready to receive affection.

▼▼▼▼▼▼▼▼▼▼▼▼▼▼▼▼▼▼▼

Jimmy sighed. He had just reached over to hold Miriam's hand while I was leading them in a discussion regarding intimacy. He followed the sigh with an explanation. "Sometimes she will let me hold her hand and sometimes she will pull away. When I leave for work, she will give me a quick peck on the cheek and thank me for going to work. That is all the affection I get! It is frustrating. To me she is the most beautiful woman I know. I delight in her. I admit she has reason to doubt that after I cheated on her. That was wrong, but it does not change the fact that I love her and want a full relationship with her."

Miriam graciously answered him with something like this. "I think that will come. Despite your disregard for God and me, I love you; but right now, I am not ready for intimacy on your schedule. My peck on the check is a down payment. My holding your hand at times is a down payment. I am still reeling from the shock of your choice. You can say it just happened, but that does not change the fact that it happened. I am especially unwilling to show affection in public. I am embarrassed to do so. Our friends who know what you did think I am crazy for mending this relationship. So, please be patient while I work through all the emotions and thoughts with which I am wrestling."

▲▲▲▲▲▲▲▲▲▲▲▲▲▲▲▲▲▲▲▲

STRATEGY EIGHT

Dispel Doubt with an Open Life

(Psalm 34:5; Matthew 6:19-24; 1 John 1:5-7; Ephesians 5:8-17)

Transparency diminishes your spouse's felt need to investigate. When your phone, computer, and calendar are open books, there is no need for suspicion. When you volunteer where you are going and why you are going there, you dissolve the natural panic.

As much as possible, include your spouse in your activities. One of my counselees invited his wife to travel with him on business trips. He included her in conversations and encouraged her to become good acquaintances with the women in his business circle.

Remember, you have no privacy. The two of you have become one. Give your spouse access to bills, bank accounts, and any other part of your life that he or she desires. Provide explanations for anything that your spouse questions. You will likely find that the desire for information will begin to diminish as you provide an open hand policy.

If it is necessary to travel for your job, give your spouse an invitation to call at any time day or night. Also give two or three same sex friends, like a Sunday School teacher or neighbor, the freedom to call any time they desire. Refuse to have business meals with just you and an opposite sex associate. Insist that there be a third party at all such meals.

▼▼▼▼▼▼▼▼▼▼▼▼▼▼▼▼▼▼

Recently one of the couples who conduct premarital counseling for us had a case in which both people had experienced cheating spouses in a prior marriage. The counseling couple quickly discovered that the woman, who had controlling tendencies, was overwhelmed with the fear of infidelity. The man was a relaxed, easygoing individual who tended to be impulsive. He made decisions on the fly. His job did not demand a tight schedule and he enjoyed spontaneity. Her fearfulness drove her to question his faithfulness during their engagement.

The counseling couple pointed out this discord as a red flag for the relationship. They counseled her regarding her tendency to control. They challenged him to practice transparency, recognizing her legitimate struggles. They encouraged them to postpone the marriage until they successfully grew the relationship beyond suspicion, control, and frustration.

▲▲▲▲▲▲▲▲▲▲▲▲▲▲▲▲▲▲▲▲▲

STRATEGY NINE

Dissipate Stress by Wise Choices

(Romans 12:18; Proverbs 17:14, 26-28; Proverbs 18)

Stress generates tension, which puts nerves on edge. Discovery of unfaithfulness (whether a physical or an emotional affair) engenders high levels of stress. Once it is out in the open and you have hashed it out, do not assume that your spouse has moved on. He or she is thinking about it every waking hour. Dissipate his or her stress level by making wise choices in what you expect from your spouse.

Be careful to make choices that will not communicate that friends, activities, or even children have priority over your spouse. To do so will fan the stress level.

Avoid all references to the attractiveness of the opposite sex. Even something as benign as looking through a high school yearbook and noting how cute or handsome someone was can remind your spouse that the appearance or prowess of others attracts you.

Honest discussion of differences is necessary. Beware of arguing—having to win. It opens the door to say words that you wish you could recall. Make it your purpose to speak words that encourage and uplift your spouse (Ephesians 4:29).

When having an affair, you found a variety of ways to make time to be with and do things with that person. When you cannot find the time to do something your spouse desires to do, or you choose not to engage in an activity because it is not something you like to do, you generate stress for your spouse. It says, "You are not important enough for me to make the time to engage in or learn to enjoy the activity you want to do." Maybe the two of you never played checkers or built a puzzle together. Maybe that is one of those small indicators of what went wrong and positioned you for the affair.

▼▼▼▼▼▼▼▼▼▼▼▼▼▼▼▼▼▼

Charlie had a deep-sea fishing trip with the men of his family scheduled in nine months. His "ugly indiscretion" as his wife called the affair that occurred four months ago transpired at the company picnic where the beer ran freely. Charlie and Martha reverted to the old high school lifestyle at the picnic and joined the crowd. Martha realized that Charlie's "ugly indiscretion" was the result of drunkenness.

Martha was very aware that the men of Charlie's family would have lots of beer on the trip Charlie was planning to go on with them. She warned him, "Don't go on that trip!"

Charlie was sorry for his affair. "I did not even think the woman was attractive," he said with a measure of disgust. He had come to counseling to get the counselor to convince Martha that this was a family tradition, and there was no reason to be concerned because there would be no women there. At the end of an hour session and walking through a biblical understanding of marriage and faithfulness, the counselor concluded by saying, "Charlie, your male family tradition is not as important as Martha's peace of mind. For her sake and in the best interest of your marriage, I recommend that you obey the Scripture and exercise love for your wife by giving her preference (Romans 12:8). You must avoid even the appearance of evil if you are going to rebuild her trust and your marriage."

▲▲▲▲▲▲▲▲▲▲▲▲▲▲▲▲▲▲

STRATEGY TEN
Dispense with Facebook, Twitter, and Instagram

In my experience, these electronic means of communication—Facebook, Twitter, and Instagram—have shown up as a trust-breaker in multiple counseling cases over the past several years. Perhaps this form of communication has not been an issue in your situation. Dispense with it anyway, at least until your relationship is renewed, as a demonstration of your commitment to rebuilding trust.

It would not be unusual when you break off the relationship for that "significant other" to use Facebook[4] to get at your spouse. It is a great tool to spread gossip.

In addition, when you are at an emotional low because your spouse has temporarily pulled back from you, it is easy to spew your guts to a same sex Facebook friend only to have someone else pick it up and funnel it back to your spouse. Facebook is not the place for you to emote. You may need one trusted friend with whom you can share your lows, but ensure it is a friend who will not commiserate with you. You need a friend who will listen and then remind you from Scripture of how you need to be thinking and acting (Galatians 6:1-2).

---

[4] I am using Facebook as a euphemism for the various electronic means of communication.

▼▼▼▼▼▼▼▼▼▼▼▼▼▼▼▼▼▼▼

Recently, I finished a marital counseling case in which the wife had engaged in an affair. We were meeting for our termination session. The positive spiritual, personal, and relational dynamics were satisfying and beyond what one would have expected in such cases. During this final session, I looked at the husband and asked, "Is there anything that we need to put on the table and discuss?" He hesitated, looked at her and then back to me. "Well, there was this posting by her friend on Facebook that concerned me." The wife had objected to discontinuing Facebook so they agreed on the compromise of having a joint Facebook account. We sorted this out and it was innocent. However, I used the occasion to recount for them the number of cases we have seen in which an electronic medium has been the catalyst of marital discord. I cited a statistic from current social research indicating that a high number of affairs have been traced back to old flames reconnecting in this manner. The medium is not evil, but for a troubled marriage, it can very easily become the platform for evil.

▲▲▲▲▲▲▲▲▲▲▲▲▲▲▲▲▲▲▲

STRATEGY ELEVEN
Engage in a Spiritual Journey

If you have had an affair (emotional or physical) you have not been walking a spiritual journey with Jesus or your spouse. Jesus put it this way, *As the Father has loved me, so have I loved you. Abide in my love. If you keep my commandments, you will abide in my love, just as I have kept my Father's commandments and abide in his love* (John 15:9-10). The lifestyle that leads to sexual immorality is not a lifestyle that is abiding in Jesus. Interestingly, Jesus illustrated the idea of intimacy by describing the relationship between Himself and the Father (John 15). Paul made it very clear that we cannot abide in fellowship with God if we are walking in sexual sin (1 Thessalonians 4:3-8).

Assure your spouse that you desire to spend time with him or her considering the Word of God together and engaging in mutual prayer. However, do not be shocked if the first time you propose or request to do so you get rebuffed—maybe rather firmly. Respond patiently, something like this, "I understand your reaction. Please pray about it. I will ask again in about a week. I will be more than receptive any time you desire to engage on the spiritual journey with me. I am deeply sorrowed that it is only after I have failed you so miserably that I have a desire to journey with you."

He or she may not desire to attend church with you if your sin is public. Be patient and agree to temporarily attend elsewhere. However, assure your spouse that you intend to be in a good church every Sunday unless you are ill. Assure your spouse that you realize the importance of being members in good standing who are engaging in learning and serving together in a church (Hebrews 10:25).

▼▼▼▼▼▼▼▼▼▼▼▼▼▼▼▼▼▼▼

Having conducted a counseling ministry in three large churches over the past thirty-plus years, I have seen numerous couples like Harry and Linda who were in a second marriage. They were members of a prestigious Presbyterian church. Unfortunately, church was a cultural tradition. Harry was not a believer. Growing out of the stress of their marital struggles, Linda had recently trusted in Christ. A business friend led Harry to genuine faith and recommended they come for counseling. They did. Both began to grow in their faith and in their marital relationship. When they completed counseling, Harry asked, "Could I come to the Lay Counselor Training Class?" He did. Over the next year, they became fully engaged in the church and the ministry. Their marriage flourished, and they influenced other marriages for good.

▲▲▲▲▲▲▲▲▲▲▲▲▲▲▲▲▲▲▲▲

STRATEGY TWELVE

Rebuilding Trust Flows from Rebuilding the Relationship: Remember, Repent, Revive

(Proverbs 5; Song of Solomon; Revelation 2:1-7)

In the letter to the Ephesian church, Jesus gave us a great outline for restoring a marriage. Affairs, like algae, flourish in stagnation. No one wants to swim in a stagnated lake or pool, whether a church fellowship or a marriage, it is the same. That is what happened in that early church—they lost their first love. When we lose that first love, we start looking elsewhere for the stimulation that love brings. Therefore, the first instruction of Jesus to remember fits both His church and your marriage. *Remember* all that you put into that relationship to generate that first love.

The first thing you did to begin rebuilding trust was to own your sin and repent. Now you must repent of your disregard of the marriage relationship. You chose to act on your personal discontent in your marriage. You need to seek forgiveness for your neglect and the abandonment of your wedding vow affirmed to God and your spouse when asked, "... will you fulfill this covenant with God by loving, honoring, comforting, and cherishing her from this day forward, forsaking all others, keeping only unto her for as long as you both shall live?" Therefore, the second instruction is to *repent*!

The third instruction is to *revive* what you had. This starts with a grateful spirit expressed to your spouse for his or her commitment to remain in the marriage. Your spouse has demonstrated the height of love in making that decision. Yes, there will be times when you will feel your spouse's wrath—anger, unpredictable moods, crying, withdrawal, and reluctance to re-engage sexually. Remember, your spouse is human, and a sinner, so cut your spouse some slack and practice that aspect of the fruit of the Spirit called *longsuffering*. Frequently express your gratitude for a second chance.

Perhaps in better days the two of you enjoyed going out to dinner or attending certain community events. Reviving the relationship will include enjoying these again. However, it may be wise to find new venues; old ones may stir mixed emotions. Re-engage in activities of mutual enjoyment and create new memories and experiences. Explore places together. If your spouse requests visiting a place with memories from the past, do so, but let your spouse take the lead on talking about what this place or activity meant to him or her.

As the negative emotions diminish, let your spouse know that you understand that engaging in any physical intimacy must be at his or her discretion. Restoring intimacy is essential; God has bestowed this unique dimension upon marriage. Nevertheless, you have tainted it with your disrespect and your distain for its sanctity. Your spouse must determine the rate of restoration. For some people, this comes quickly and seems to be the catalyst to move the relationship forward. For others, it takes weeks or even months of patient, gentle kindness. For some people, sexuality in the marriage does not seem to be about trust, yet for others it is all about trust.

Verbal affirmation of love needs to be frequent. Most likely, you can identify your spouse's desired manner for receiving love. It may be gifts or time or talking. Whatever else it may be, a genuine and frequent "I love you" is essential.

▼▼▼▼▼▼▼▼▼▼▼▼▼▼▼▼▼▼▼

I once interviewed a couple who recovered from a double affair. We sat across the table at a nice restaurant. I listened to their story of how they learned to trust each other. However, for the most part, I watched them. Their love for each other flowed from their eyes. At the time of the interview, they were in their early to mid-sixties—more than thirty years after the affairs.

▲▲▲▲▲▲▲▲▲▲▲▲▲▲▲▲▲▲▲

STRATEGY THIRTEEN

Trust Can Flourish in Worshiping and Ministering Together

God refers to us as sheep. Sheep need a shepherd to care for them. Many of the counselees I see have failed to acknowledge that they are sheep in need of the shepherd's care. When Psalm 23 is quoted, most respond knowingly. Yet when asked how it applies to them, they sputter. That Jesus refers to Himself as the Good Shepherd is vaguely familiar. Peter's reference to Jesus as the Great Shepherd is even less familiar. When asked just how these images apply to them with an affair-torn marriage suffering broken trust, they respond with a blank stare.

If you are members of a well-grounded Bible teaching church, skip down to number seven. If you are not members of a well-grounded Bible teaching church, find one and join. To accomplish this step, you will need to do several things.

1. Pray together for wisdom in choosing a church.
2. Prepare a list of churches within a ten-mile radius of your home.
3. Go to the website of each church and read it together.
4. Listen to three recent consecutive sermons and ask these questions.
    a. Did the speaker explain the text of the Bible to which he referred?
    b. Did the speaker explain the continuity of the text from one week to the next?
    c. Did the speaker suggest how you can apply or implement the message in your life?

5. Once you believe a church is a Bible teaching church, make three consecutive visits.
6. Make an appointment to interview the pastor. At the end of the interview, explain your life journey and ask if he is comfortable with your joining the church.
7. Now that you have found a good church, become involved in three ways.
   a. Be faithful in attending Sunday Worship and Sunday School weekly.
   b. Become involved in a small group.
   c. Volunteer to serve in an activity where you can serve together. This may be as simple as volunteering for the Greeter Team that welcomes folks on a Sunday morning.

Conclusion

In these pages, we have attempted to deal honestly with emotional responses. Few people betrayed by an affair will respond according to the Christian ideal. When they do, they are likely being dishonest with themselves or the offending spouse. Betrayal hurts, and it hurts deeply! It resembles a tornado ripping through a community. There is much destruction; however, there are structures that are virtually untouched or only slightly damaged. The latter provide points of hope. The foundations remain. For the Christian, those foundations are primarily spiritual in nature. The indwelling of the Holy Spirit makes His fruit possible: love, expressed in joy, peace, patience, longsuffering, etc. (Galatians 5:22ff). This fruit can enable the offended to forgive and trust while the offender can be repentant and patient.

> You cheated once. You were graced with forgiveness.
> Presuming you will be forgiven again is to play the fool.
> God is able to enable your spouse to forgive again.
> Don't assume that your spouse will choose to do so.

Rebuilding the Relationship After the Affair

JESUS' SOLUTION FOR REBUILDING THE RELATIONSHIP

Now that we have laid out the strategies for rebuilding trust, let us turn our attention to rebuilding the relationship. In our previous discussions we noted Jesus' exhortation in Revelation 2:1-7 where Jesus set before His church at Ephesus to rebuild their relationship with Him. He sets out three simple steps: First, remember what you had and what you did that cultivated the relationship. Second, repent of what you did and what you did not do that was destructive to the relationship. Third, revive those thoughts and actions that shaped the original rich relationship.

A study of the book of Ephesians will call to mind what Jesus did to initiate their relationship as well as the life-style response of the congregation that contributed to their vibrant relationship with Him. In the letter Jesus later sent to this church (Revelation 2:1-7), He describes their demise. Here is what Jesus says:

> *To the angel of the church in Ephesus write: "The words of him who holds the seven stars in his right hand, who walks among the seven golden lampstands.*
> *I know your works, your toil and your patient endurance, and how you cannot bear with those who are evil, but have tested those who call themselves apostles and are not, and found them to be false. I know you are enduring patiently and bearing up for my name's sake, and you have not grown weary.*
> **But I have this against you, that you have abandoned the love you had at first.**

Remember therefore from where you have fallen; repent, and do the works you did at first. If not, I will come to you and remove your lampstand from its place, unless you repent. Yet this you have: you hate the works of the Nicolaitans, which I also hate. He who has an ear, let him hear what the Spirit says to the churches. To the one who conquers I will grant to eat of the tree of life, which is in the paradise of God."

A wife or a husband could write a letter to the offending spouse and include the words, "I have this against you; you have abandoned the love you had at first." Certainly, when there has been an affair this is true.

▼▼▼▼▼▼▼▼▼▼▼▼▼▼▼▼▼▼

Jack and Rosemary moved to Johnson City and joined the First Presbyterian Church. They also began attending the Lamplighters Sunday School class, a class of young couples starting their families. George and Susie, whose parents lived a thousand miles away, invited Jack and Rosemary to spend Thanksgiving Day with them. This began a robust friendship that both couples enjoyed. Rosemary later referred to this friendship as a "summer romance." It was both a sweet and bitter reference because the rapidly developing relationships subsequently turned sour.

Both marriage relationships had grown cold, though both couples had been married only a few years. As a result, George and Rosemary clicked. It was not long before they began emailing and meeting for lunch since they both worked downtown in the same office building. Both were attorneys and avid tennis players. Neither of their spouses knew much about the law and neither played tennis. Before long George and Rosemary's friendship deteriorated into an emotionally intimate relationship, though their Christian convictions kept it from becoming sexual.

▲▲▲▲▲▲▲▲▲▲▲▲▲▲▲▲▲▲▲▲

With this vignette in mind, consider Jesus' parable of the Prodigal Son (Luke 15:11-32). The prodigal's relationship with his father was in the "pig pen." In Jesus' story, the prodigal took stock of his circumstances as well as the shattered bond with his father. He recalled the benefits and blessings of their former relationship and his heart was changed. With the prodigal's repentance and desire for a renewed relationship, along with the father's acceptance and forgiveness, the parable ends well.

▼▼▼▼▼▼▼▼▼▼▼▼▼▼▼▼▼▼▼▼

Jack and Rosemary's and George and Susie's relationships were also in the "pig pen." However, God granted repentance (2 Timothy 2:25, 26). For George and Susie, God worked as the counselor skillfully helping the couple weave a beautiful tapestry of remembrance. He guided them in recalling varied experiences and values in their early relationship. He coached George through the process of remembering what had attracted him to Susie. During this process, George's regret and repentance were almost overwhelming. As Susie observed this, her heart softened, and she confessed that over the years she had become resentful because George was not the strong leader she had thought he would be. As a result, she had withdrawn and shut him out of her decision-making. Through a reconciliation session with a pastor, both George and Susie came to repentance. Following this session, they began to reproduce the actions that had contributed to their original tender relationship. They prayed together. They physically hugged each other. They wept together, and they began speaking in affectionate tones.

▲▲▲▲▲▲▲▲▲▲▲▲▲▲▲▲▲▲▲▲

Over the months of counseling, each couple in the vignette recognized that their marital relationship did not reflect the love they had enjoyed during their courtship. Their counselor helped them revive this first love through the following six initiatives:

RELATING—No relationship grows without relating. Relating takes time. We cannot say, "OK, we have ten minutes, let's relate and develop our intimacy." This does not work with Jesus and this does not work with your spouse.

INVESTING—Sometimes we have the time, but no energy left for relating. It takes energy to enjoy each other, to do things together. Just as we must invest energy and time in Bible study and prayer to renew a passion for Jesus, it takes investing time and energy to create a passionate intimacy with your spouse. Investing takes intentionality. It means giving your mate priority.

LISTENING—To know someone, it is necessary to attentively listen to his or her heart. Listening to God requires exercising a quiet spirit before him as you meditate on His Word. Listening to your spouse requires a patient and gentle spirit to hear the heart—those deep emotions: fear, anxiety, desires, dreams, and hurts—without reacting negatively.

GIVING—Intimacy involves giving ourselves to the other person. Jesus puts it this way in John 15:4: *"Abide in Me, and I in you."* It means sacrificing our desires to minister to the desires of the other; whether for Jesus or my spouse, the principle is the same.

CARING—Intimacy involves practicing tender-heartedness. This word entails concern for the feelings of the other person. It means I avoid words and actions that disappoint Jesus because I do not want to grieve the Holy Spirit Who lives within. It means restraining my speech and actions to treat and speak to my spouse with concern for the impact I will have on him or her (Galatians 5:26; Ephesians 4:32)

FORGIVING—Forgiveness is essential. It clears away the hurts and rubble of broken promises and wounding actions. God offers forgiveness to us and instructs us to give it to each other. I frequently invite my counselees to climb onto God's bulldozer and to clear the debris by choosing to forgive, thereby clearing the way to rebuild.

Therefore, what steps can you incorporate into your journey together that will foster these necessary initiatives for rebuilding a strong marriage that becomes affair proof? Allow me to suggest the following steps.

INITIATIVES: Ten Practical Steps

1. Review Strategy Thirteen in the first section of this book (p. 45) regarding spiritual development.
2. Develop a list of the meaningful actions your spouse did early in your marriage that delighted your heart.
3. Develop a list of the actions you did early in the relationship to express your love for your spouse.
4. Share these lists with each other and then memorialize the lists as stones of remembrance and guideposts for the future.

5. Establish a regular date night—engage in something that you both enjoy doing without children and that lasts for at least two hours. Keep a journal of your dates and highlight the ones you enjoy most.
6. Read at least one book a year about marriage and discuss it. Read a chapter a month and set aside a time to go to breakfast, or Sunday lunch, or on a hike (you get the idea) when you can discuss the current chapter.
7. Take a mini-vacation (Thursday night through Sunday noon) without children twice a year. Include in this weekend:
   a. At least one special dinner in a romantic setting.
   b. At least two opportunities to have a lingering love-making time and focus on pleasing your spouse.
   c. A two-hour session over lunch when you review your goals of the past six months and evaluate how you achieved them or what interfered with achieving those you did not get accomplished. Remember the initiatives above and practice them during this discussion. Do not argue!
   d. At least one physical activity together each day—hike, tennis, swim, 5-K run, etc.
   e. At least twenty to thirty minutes to write down prayer requests and take turns praying for these concerns and each other.
   f. Time to read a passage of Scripture and discuss it before or after prayer time
8. Make a list of the argument starters for you (e.g., where we will spend Christmas, how much we will spend on presents for Christmas and birthdays, when and where we will vacation, etc.) and plan appropriate

times to discuss these items while keeping in mind the initiatives above.
9. Practice saying, "I am so sorry; I sinned. Please forgive me."
10. Speak the truth in love (Ephesians 4:15). Recently an article that examined secular factors contributing to the marital success of Evangelical Christians came to my attention. The researchers drew several important conclusions, including the following:

> "Communication therefore plays a critical role in a couple's ability to achieve a successful marriage ... couples who over-saturate their marriage with positivity and avoidance are more likely to experience conflict and lower levels of marital satisfaction than couples who embrace negativity [disagreement] and diversity [different desires, visions, expectations]. When it comes to communication among couples, the most important thing is that spouses actually communicate, whether it is positive or negative."[5]

Therefore, facilitate a positive atmosphere by practicing the following five rules of communication based upon Ephesians 4:25-32.

---

[5] Nick T. Ogle and Monte Hasz. *Secular Factors Contributing to Marital Success: A Review of Secular Factors Contributing to Marital Success with Application to Evangelical Christian Marriages*. Marriage and Family: A Christian Journal 7. No. 1 (2004). 21-32.

Paul's Rules for Maintaining A Relationship

Rule One: Stop Lying and Start Truth-Telling

When you are feeling hurt and your spouse asks, "What's wrong?" what is your likely answer? "Oh, it is nothing!"

▼▼▼▼▼▼▼▼▼▼▼▼▼▼▼▼▼▼▼▼

Charles asked his wife if she had some cash he could use for lunch. When Sandy asked Charles, "What happened to the twenty-five dollars you had in your pocket yesterday?" he responded, "Oh, forget it, I'm good." He lied by evading her question as he walked out the door.

▲▲▲▲▲▲▲▲▲▲▲▲▲▲▲▲▲▲▲▲

▼▼▼▼▼▼▼▼▼▼▼▼▼▼▼▼▼▼▼▼

Mary watched the mail and made sure she pulled the Macy's statement. She did not want to face Sam's reaction to her recent shoe purchase. Mary lied with her *sleight of hand*!

▲▲▲▲▲▲▲▲▲▲▲▲▲▲▲▲▲▲▲▲

Your spouse is your closest neighbor. If there is anywhere that speaking the truth is essential, it is within marriage. Practice assiduously laying aside falsehood and diligently speaking the truth.

Rule Two: Be Relationship-Focused Not Issue-Focused: Stay current!

Most people read Ephesians 4:26 and say, "If we tried to settle an issue over which we were arguing before we went to bed, it would be 2:00-3:00 in the morning and we'd finally give up without having settled it." The problem is, each has been selfishly *issue-focused* and not other-oriented or *relationship-focused*. There are times when you will not be able to close an issue. You may not have the information needed, or you may be too frustrated over the situation to address it without hurting one another.

In this verse, Paul is not speaking of the *issue*, he is speaking of the *relationship*. Confess your mean-spirited speech and seek forgiveness for your verbal attack. Volunteer to lay aside the issue. Ask your spouse if you can pray together and agree to address the issue later. This is a way to avoid unnecessary conflict out of emotions.

If you go to bed angry, how likely are you to awake either angry or depressed? Either way Paul warns that you will give Satan the advantage (v. 27). You will start the day on edge. It will only take the slightest frustration to revive the attitude and the argument of the night before.

RULE THREE: Attack the Problem Not Your Spouse

The best translation of the word *unwholesome* (Ephesians 4:29) is the colloquialism *cutting*.

Put-Off: Do not allow any cutting word to come out of your mouth!

Put-On: Speak words that will edify, that is, build up and minister to your spouse at the very point where you want to cut him or her down. When you want to say, "What were you thinking, you idiot!" replace it with "You must have felt awful at that point. I am so sorry you had that struggle."

Grease your relationship with grace! Do not gum it up with verbal dust and debris. Notice Paul's footnote—grieve not the Spirit. Perhaps I can contrast verse 27 with verse 30 this way: Do not give the devil an opportunity but do give the Spirit opportunity. By choosing to speak in a manner that attacks the problem rather than choosing to speak words that attack your spouse, you listen to the Spirit. Thereby you give the Spirit opportunity to bless your relationship rather than giving Satan the opportunity to once more be about dismantling your relationship. (See the Appendix on p. 67.)

RULE FOUR: Do Not React, Do Pro-Act

Do not react (Ephesians 4:31)! Note again, the *Put-Off* and *Put-On* dynamic along with renewed thinking (v. 22-24). The reactions listed in verse 31 are progressive. If you do not put off the bitterness (a settled attitude of anger driven by unforgiveness), it will give way to wrath (inward agitation), which will give way to anger (the outward expression of that inward agitation). The anger, unchecked, will proceed to clamor (loud yelling) and we have all observed that clamor leads to slander or character assassination. In the original language, the word *slander* is *blasphemy*. Therefore, character assassination equates with debasing God since you debase a person who is created in God's image. God says this will give way to malice (intent to do harm). Forgiveness[6] and moving past the past are essential for clearing the heart of bitterness and its concomitants that stymie effective communication.

Do pro-act (v. 32)! Be kind and gentle. Hold back your desire to hurt and, instead, treat your spouse as God has treated you. Be tenderhearted. Remember Jesus as He spoke to Mary and Martha. He wept and expressed concern for them in their suffering even though He was frustrated with their being slow of understanding (John 11:18-27).

---

[6] A fellow counselor who reviewed this manuscript wrote this note to me. "I do not believe you have been direct enough with the 'innocent' party, i.e., the one who was sinned against. While it will probably be the hardest thing she will ever do in her life, she has a responsibility before God to forgive and work hard at restoration—even going against her feelings. She is obliged to remember that she was forgiven a great debt herself and now has a responsibility to forgive the much smaller debt (by comparison) owed by her husband (as per Jesus' parable in Matthew 18). I would agree with him. However, the emphasis in this booklet is upon the offender and therefore I did not do as he suggested. If you are the offended party, I would urge you to humbly consider this point.

The positive actions described by the *Put-On* dynamic embody the process of renewing the mind. Only as the mind is renewed by the Word of God are we able to choose to respond positively to challenging interpersonal situations. Note that God is the model—be forgiving as God in Christ has forgiven you. In Romans 2:1-4 Paul clearly instructs us with the knowledge that generates this renewed thinking. He teaches us how God demonstrates tolerance and patience by withholding the wrath we deserve. His goodness is that we have not experienced the judgment we deserve, and this goodness and kindness leads us to repentance. This renewed thinking enables us to *Pro-Act* and choose not to *React* as we give our spouse the opportunity to come to repentance in the existential situation. It is what empowers us to forgive, to treat with kindness and to think more about the other person's feelings not winning our point.

Forgiving is God's D-12 Bulldozer, the largest bulldozer made. It clears away the sin of every believer with one fell swoop. It made it possible for God to apply that forgiveness to each of us as the Spirit brought us to repentance. Likewise, we need to keep the bulldozer running in our hearts to be used at a moment's notice to clear the debris of offense even as God does according to 1 John 1:9. If you ask, "What if my spouse does not repent?" Peter supplies the answer, *Love covers a multitude of sins* (1 Peter 4:8). Love decides to forgive and treats with love so that when repentance occurs, it is ready to respond with a verbal "I forgive you." In the meantime, that internal forgiveness protects you from developing the bitterness referenced in verse 31.

RULE FIVE: Listen Before You Speak or Get Angry[7]
(James 1:19-20)

The Apostle James adds a fifth rule, *Know this, my beloved brothers: let every person be quick to hear, slow to speak, slow to anger; for the anger of man does not produce the righteousness of God.* This is instructive, especially in emotionally tense situations. If you are the offended spouse, listen carefully; ask for time to process what you heard and set aside your first response (usually anger). Then when you have prayed and processed what you have been told, list your questions and return to the conversation. Speak slowly and deliberately so you can sort out the incident or situation.

If you are the offender, and your spouse questions your actions or attitudes, listen! Do not be fashioning your defense. Resist the frustration that leads to anger because your mate is once again questioning you. Speak slowly and thoughtfully with his or her hurt in mind. Be praying for wisdom to determine how you can minister to him or her.

We have not covered all that God teaches us about communication. However, we have covered five rules you can memorize and determine to weave into the fabric of your life. In doing so, you will certainly enhance your recovery from the affair and acquire the tools to prevent much of the static that has contributed to your previous poor communication and marital breakdown. These five rules provide the structure that enables couples to process the negatives that will occur in every marriage in a context that is positive. The wise God of the Judeo-Christian heritage Who

---

[7] The first four rules appeared in *Three To Get Ready: A Premarital Counseling Manual*. They appear here slightly revised and expanded. I have subsequently added rule five in my counseling practice.

ordained marriage through His Word provided the instruction manual for marriage. We do well to avail ourselves of His loving instructions.

Our Strong Suggestion

If you have engaged in a physical affair, we strongly suggest that you volunteer to be tested for a sexually transmitted disease (STD) before re-engaging physically with your spouse. To volunteer to undergo this test affirms that you understand the gravity of your sin, and it affirms that you value the well-being of your spouse.

If your spouse has engaged in a physical affair and has not volunteered to be tested for an STD, it is appropriate for you to make this request before re-engaging in a physical relationship. This request is the exercise of good stewardship of your body, the temple of the Holy Spirit (1 Corinthians 6:15-20). It also affirms that you love your spouse enough to protect your welfare for the long-term duration of the marriage.

APPENDIX

OTHER IMPORTANT DIAGNOSTIC AND PRESCRIPTIVE TEXTS

James 4:1

James gives us the diagnosis of the root cause of most angry arguments. *What causes quarrels and what causes fights among you? Is it not this, that your passions are at war within you?* Angry arguments most always are rooted in self-focus:

>I know I am right.
>I know what is best.
>I know we cannot afford that.
>I am not going to do that.

Proverbs 29:11

Proverbs clearly reflects our options when our spouse is angrily expressing his or her selfishness.

>*A fool gives full vent to his spirit, but a wise man quietly holds it back.*

We can blow up or we can restrain our reaction and choose to respond gracefully.

James 1:19-20 complements **Proverbs 15:1**

James tells how to respond to' avoid these angry situations:

>*Know this, my beloved brothers: let every person be quick to hear, slow to speak, slow to anger; for the anger of man does not produce the righteousness of God.*

Proverbs prescribes how to express our response to produce the righteousness of God:

> *A gentle answer turns away wrath, but a harsh word stirs up anger.*

Proverbs 16:32

Proverbs presents us with a contrast that should get our attention:

> *Whoever is slow to anger is better than the mighty, and he who rules his spirit than he who takes a city.*

So, we conclude, even when you are upset and angry, focus on the *relationship* not the *issue* and treat your spouse with respect:

- **Personally**—Guard the manner of your speech to your spouse.
- **Intellectually**—Listen and give your spouse the opportunity to express their ideas.
- **Spiritually**—Seek to pray with your spouse over difficult issues and seek to examine issues together utilizing Scripture and godly counsel.

About the Authors

Dr. Howard Eyrich's career has spanned more than sixty years. He has filled various roles including seminary professor and president, pastor and church planter. He retired as the Director of Counseling Ministries at Briarwood Presbyterian Church, Birmingham, Alabama.

He has served on the boards of the Association of Certified Biblical Counselors, Birmingham Theological Seminary, Trinity Seminary, Master's International University of Divinity, the Biblical Counseling Coalition, and The Owen Center; as well as various Presbytery and Presbyterian Church in America denominational committees, to name the major efforts.

His publishing efforts include two books as solo author, three books with a co-author, and numerous chapters in significant volumes in the biblical counseling field, as well as articles for *The Journal of Biblical Counseling* and several other magazines.

Dr. Eyrich and his wife Pamela have two grown children, eight grandchildren and one great-grandchild. Retirement for him is a time for ministry. He writes, teaches, preaches, and travels for the Kingdom. He also enjoys the hobbies of model railroading, hunting, and shooting.

Dr. Eyrich is available to speak in conferences, fill pulpits, and for intensive marriage interventions, especially with ministries' couples.

Follow Howard Eyrich
Facebook: facebook.com/howardeyrich
Twitter: Howard Eyrich @earkie1
Instagram: Howard Eyrich @earkie1
Amazon: http://amzn.to/2wSR9FF
Blog: howardeyrich.com

Dr. Cheryl Blackmon is a certified counselor with The Association of Certified Biblical Counselors. She holds an MA and EdD in education. Before beginning her career as a Biblical Counselor, Cheryl served as principal of a 1000 student private Christian elementary school where she logged many hours counseling students, parents, and faculty. She recently retired as the Coordinator of the Biblical Counseling and Women and Children's Counselor at Briarwood Counseling Ministry where she worked closely with Dr. Eyrich including frequently teaming to co-counsel a number of family counseling cases.

ALSO BY DR. HOWARD EYRICH

A Call to Christian Patriotism: A Weekly Devotional Essay Series – Howard A. Eyrich, Focus Publishing, Bemidji, MN, 2012.

Christian Decision Making and the Will of God: A Practical Model – Howard Eyrich, KDP, 2014

Curing the Heart: A Model for Biblical Counseling – Howard Eyrich & William Hines, Christian Focus Publications, 2014.

Grief: Learning to Live with Loss – Howard A. Eyrich, P & R Publishing, 2010

Hope and Help for the Suffering – Howard Eyrich & Howard Dial, Focus Publishing, Bemidji, MN, 2010.

Hope and Help for the Homosexual – Howard Eyrich & Howard Dial, Focus Publishing, Bemidji, MN, 2011.

Hope for New Beginnings—Dr. Howard Eyrich and Shirley Crowder, Growth Advantage Communication LLC, 2017.

Paul the Counselor: Disciple-making as Modeled by the Apostle – edited by Bill Hines & Mark Shaw (Chapters 7 & 12), Focus Publishing, Bemidji, MN, 2014.

The Art of Aging: A Christian Handbook – Howard Eyrich, – Howard A. Eyrich, Focus Publishing, Bemidji, MN, 2012.

Three to Get Ready: Premarital Counseling Manual, 2nd Edition – Howard Eyrich, Focus Publishing, Bemidji, MN, 1996.

Totally Sufficient: The Bible and Christian Counseling, Revised – Ed Hindson & Howard Eyrich, Christian Focus Publishing, 2004.

Scripture References

Old Testament

Psalm 1:1-2	p. 19
Psalm 23	p. 45
Psalm 34:5	p. 34
Psalm 26:6-7	p. 26
Psalm 27:13-14	p. 26
Psalm 51:6	p. 16
Psalm 51:10	p. 16
Proverbs 1:20-33	p. 30
Proverbs 2:1-22	p. 29
Proverbs 5	p. 42
Proverbs 5:1-14	p. 30
Proverbs 13:15	p. 28
Proverbs 13:21	p. 29
Proverbs 12:22	p. 16
Proverbs 14:12	p. 18
Proverbs 15:1	p. 67
Proverbs 16:32	p. 68
Proverbs 17:14	p. 36
Proverbs 17:26-28	p. 36
Proverbs 18	p. 36
Proverbs 18:13	p. 28
Proverbs 21:24	p. 21
Proverbs 26:4-5	p. 21
Proverbs 28:13	p. 16
Proverbs 29:11	p. 67
Song of Solomon	p. 42
Zechariah 8:15-17	p. 24

New Testament

Matthew 5:23-24	p. 18
Matthew 5:30	p. 18
Matthew 6:19-24	p. 34
Matthew 18	p. 62
Matthew 18:8	p. 20
Mark 9:43	p. 19
Luke 15:11-32	p. 53
John 11:18-27	p. 62
John 15	p. 40
John 15:4	p. 54
John 15:9-10	p. 40
Romans 2:1-4	p. 63
Romans 12:3	p. 30
Romans 12:8	p. 37
Romans 12:16-18	p. 24
Romans 12:18	p. 36
Romans 12:21	p. 25
1 Corinthians 6:15-20	p. 66
1 Corinthians 13:4-8	p. 26
Galatians 5:22	p. 26 & 47
Galatians 5:26	p. 55
Galatians 6:1-2	p. 38
Ephesians 4:1-6	p. 31
Ephesians 4:2-3	p. 31
Ephesians 4:15	p. 57
Ephesians 4:22-24	p. 62
Ephesians 4:25-32	p. 57
Ephesians 4:25	p. 15 & 16
Ephesians 4:26	p. 60
Ephesians 4:27	p. 60 & 61
Ephesians 4:29	p. 36 & 61

New Testament (continued)

Ephesians 4:30	p. 61
Ephesians 4:31	p. 62 & 63
Ephesians 4:32	p. 55 & 62
Ephesians 5:7-16	p. 16
Ephesians 5:8-17	p. 19 & 34
Philippians 1:9-11	p. 28
Philippians 2:1-7	p. 28
Colossians 3:12-17	p. 31
1 Thessalonians 4:3-8	p. 40
1 Thessalonians 5:22	p. 30
2 Timothy 2:22	p. 30
2 Timothy 2:25	p. 53
2 Timothy 2:26	p. 53
Hebrews 10:25	p. 41
James 1:2-4	p. 26
James 1:12-17	p. 21
James 1:19-20	p. 64 & 67
James 4:1	p. 67
James 4:1-3	p. 21
James 4:17	p. 18
James 4:5-12	p. 22
1 Peter 4:8	p. 63
1 John 1:5-7	p. 17 & 34
1 John 1:9	p. 63
Revelation 2:1-7	p. 25, 42 & 51

Published by:

Growth Advantage Communication, LLC

3867 James Hill Circle

Hoover, Alabama 35226

growthadvantage@gmail.com

CPSIA information can be obtained
at www.ICGtesting.com
Printed in the USA
LVHW040813300523
748318LV00003B/118